Verbal Reasoning Activities

Why do people carry umbrellas?

What would happen if you did not have a bed?

What happens when you eat an ice cream cone on a hot day?

Why do you think the boy is holding up his hand?

Jean Gilliam DeGaetano
Illustrated by Kevin M. Newman

Great Ideas for Teaching, Inc. • P.O. Box 444 • Wrightsville Beach, NC 28480-0444

Copyright 1998 Great Ideas for Teaching, Inc.
All rights reserved. Printed in the U.S.A.
Published by Great Ideas for Teaching, Inc.
P.O. Box 444, Wrightsville Beach, NC 28480

Copies of all materials may be produced for classroom use and homework assignments. Copies may not be produced for entire school districts, used for commercial resale, stored in a retrieval system, or transmitted in any form; electronic, mechanical, recording, etc., without permission from the publisher.

ISBN 1-886143-41-2

Verbal Reasoning Activities

By Jean Gilliam DeGaetano
Illustrations by Kevin M. Newman

The natural curiosity of small children prompts numerous "why?" questions to adults. They want to know "why" cats have claws, dogs have tails, the postman brings mail, parents go to work, lightning and thunder happen, leaves fall off trees, ice freezes, etc. The list of questions is endless. The questions both provide them with information and engage them in attentive conversations with the adult.

When an adult asks a child "why" questions, shy children or very young children usually say, "I don't know." Talkative and older preschoolers; however, begin to verbalize their reasons and may even begin asking each other questions.

This unit provides numerous visual situations to assist young children in expressing verbal reasoning skills. Eight types of questions are presented:

- What would happen if......?
- Why is this true?
- What happens when......?
- What would happen?
- Why or why not?
- Why is this happening......?
- Why do you think......?

The child's answers will reflect the child's experiences in life and should be accepted if they are appropriate. The professional can ask new questions to expand on the child's answers to encourage verbal interaction.

Some scenes may be unfamiliar to the child and will result in "I don't know" answers. This will give the professional an opportunity to provide the information to the child in the form of a question such as, "Do you think ice cubes would melt if you forgot to put them back in the freezer?"

To be successful in using the unit, the children should be capable of verbally expressing their thoughts.

Name: _____

What would happen?

Instructor's Worksheet:

DIRECTIONS: Before beginning, each student should be given a copy of the worksheet that corresponds to the instructor's worksheet. All questions are to be read aloud to the students. The illustrations visually identify the <u>subject</u> of the questions and serve as clues in remembering them, but they do not provide answers to the questions. Answering the questions requires logic, reasoning and adequate verbal skills. Students should take turns answering the questions. Answers will vary and are correct if they are logical.

What would happen?

What would happen if you forgot to water a plant?

What would happen if Dad's car tire ran over a nail?

What would happen if you left your beach towel at the beach?

What would happen if you forgot to turn on the oven to bake the cookies?

What would happen if you forgot to turn off the water in the bathtub?

What would happen if you picked a flower and forgot to put it in water?

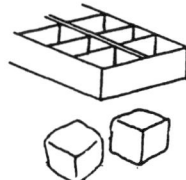

What would happen if you left ice cubes on the kitchen counter?

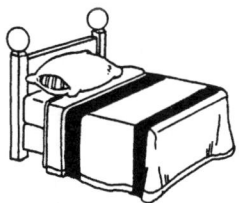

What would happen if you left your wet bathing suit on the bed?

Great Ideas for Teaching, Inc.   Verbal Reasoning Activities

Name: _____

Why?

Instructor's Worksheet:

<u>DIRECTIONS:</u> Before beginning, each student should be given a copy of the worksheet that corresponds to the instructor's worksheet. All questions are to be read aloud to the students. The illustrations visually identify the <u>subject</u> of the questions and serve as clues in remembering them, but they do not provide answers to the questions. Answering the questions requires logic, reasoning and adequate verbal skills. Students should take turns answering the questions. Answers will vary and are correct if they are logical.

Why?

Why do people put ice cubes in water?

Why do kids eat snacks?

Why do you put stamps on letters?

Why do you wrap birthday presents?

Why do people have a phone book?

Why do people lock their houses?

Why do people put curtains on their windows?

Why do people put steps on their houses?

Great Ideas for Teaching, Inc.   Page 4   Verbal Reasoning Activities

Name:_____

What would happen?

Great Ideas for Teaching, Inc.   Page 5   Verbal Reasoning Activities

Instructor's Worksheet:

DIRECTIONS: Before beginning, each student should be given a copy of the worksheet that corresponds to the instructor's worksheet. All questions are to be read aloud to the students. The illustrations visually identify the <u>subject</u> of the questions and serve as clues in remembering them, but they do not provide answers to the questions. Answering the questions requires logic, reasoning and adequate verbal skills. Students should take turns answering the questions. Answers will vary and are correct if they are logical.

What would happen?

What would happen if you left chocolate candy in the sun?

What would happen if you sat on someone's hat?

What would happen if a rope broke?

What would happen if you forgot your lunch box?

What would happen if you spilled your milk?

What would happen if you left your papers outside on a windy day?

What would happen if you picked a flower that has many thorns?

What would happen if you stepped on a crab?

Great Ideas for Teaching, Inc. — Verbal Reasoning Activities

Name:_____

What would happen?

Great Ideas for Teaching, Inc. Page 7 Verbal Reasoning Activities

Instructor's Worksheet:

DIRECTIONS: Before beginning, each student should be given a copy of the worksheet that corresponds to the instructor's worksheet. All questions are to be read aloud to the students. The illustrations visually identify the subject of the questions and serve as clues in remembering them, but they do not provide answers to the questions. Answering the questions requires logic, reasoning and adequate verbal skills. Students should take turns answering the questions. Answers will vary and are correct if they are logical.

What would happen?

What would happen if crayons were left out in the sun?

What would happen if you left a picture outside in the rain?

What would happen if you dropped a glass?

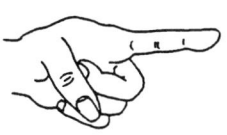
What would happen if you cut your finger?

What would happen if you missed a ball and it hit a window?

What would happen if you were on a picnic and it rained?

What would happen if you put water in a freezer?

What would happen if you lost the key to the car?

Great Ideas for Teaching, Inc.   Verbal Reasoning Activities

What happens?

Instructor's Worksheet:

DIRECTIONS: Before beginning, each student should be given a copy of the worksheet that corresponds to the instructor's worksheet. All questions are to be read aloud to the students. The illustrations visually identify the <u>subject</u> of the questions and serve as clues in remembering them, but they do not provide answers to the questions. Answering the questions requires logic, reasoning and adequate verbal skills. Students should take turns answering the questions. Answers will vary and are correct if they are logical.

What happens?

What happens when you eat an ice cream cone on a hot day?

What happens to wood when it is burned?

What happens to water when it is put in a freezer?

What happens to cookies that are baked too long?

What happens to water when it is put on a hot stove?

What happens to your hands and feet when you play in the snow?

What happens to leaves on a tree when winter comes?

What happens to snow when the sun comes out?

Great Ideas for Teaching, Inc.   <u>Verbal Reasoning Activities</u>

What can happen?

Instructor's Worksheet:

DIRECTIONS: Before beginning, each student should be given a copy of the worksheet that corresponds to the instructor's worksheet. All questions are to be read aloud to the students. The illustrations visually identify the <u>subject</u> of the questions and serve as clues in remembering them, but they do not provide answers to the questions. Answering the questions requires logic, reasoning and adequate verbal skills. Students should take turns answering the questions. Answers will vary and are correct if they are logical.

What can happen?

What can happen if you throw sand at other children?

What can happen if you let go of the handlebars of a bicycle?

What can happen if you run too fast?

What can happen if you slip on ice?

What can happen if you play too rough?

What can happen if you do not listen?

What can happen if you climb on a small branch of a tree?

What can happen if you surf in rough water?

Name: _____

Why?

Instructor's Worksheet:

DIRECTIONS: Before beginning, each student should be given a copy of the worksheet that corresponds to the instructor's worksheet. All questions are to be read aloud to the students. The illustrations visually identify the <u>subject</u> of the questions and serve as clues in remembering them, but they do not provide answers to the questions. Answering the questions requires logic, reasoning and adequate verbal skills. Students should take turns answering the questions. Answers will vary and are correct if they are logical.

Why?

Why do leaves change colors?	Why does a policeman stop traffic?
Why do you not run and yell when a baby is sleeping?	Why does a dog wag its tail?
Why do you close a window?	Why do you wash your hands before eating?
Why do you brush your teeth?	Why do people eat food?

Great Ideas for Teaching, Inc. Page 14 Verbal Reasoning Activities

Name:_____

Why?

Great Ideas for Teaching, Inc.   Verbal Reasoning Activities

Instructor's Worksheet:

DIRECTIONS: Before beginning, each student should be given a copy of the worksheet that corresponds to the instructor's worksheet. All questions are to be read aloud to the students. The illustrations visually identify the <u>subject</u> of the questions and serve as clues in remembering them, but they do not provide answers to the questions. Answering the questions requires logic, reasoning and adequate verbal skills. Students should take turns answering the questions. Answers will vary and are correct if they are logical.

Why?

Great Ideas for Teaching, Inc.   Verbal Reasoning Activities

Name:_____

Why or why not?

Great Ideas for Teaching, Inc.   Page 17   <u>Verbal Reasoning Activities</u>

Instructor's Worksheet:

DIRECTIONS: Before beginning, each student should be given a copy of the worksheet that corresponds to the instructor's worksheet. All questions are to be read aloud to the students. The illustrations visually identify the <u>subject</u> of the questions and serve as clues in remembering them, but they do not provide answers to the questions. Answering the questions requires logic, reasoning and adequate verbal skills. Students should take turns answering the questions. Answers will vary and are correct if they are logical.

Why or why not?

Why does a dog make a good pet?	Why does an elephant not make a good pet?
Why does a cat make a good pet?	Why does a snake not make a good pet?
Why does a bird make a good pet?	Why does a rhinoceros not make a good pet?
Why does a horse make a good pet?	Why does a tiger not make a good pet?

Great Ideas for Teaching, Inc.   Verbal Reasoning Activities

Name:_____

Why?

Instructor's Worksheet:

DIRECTIONS: Before beginning, each student should be given a copy of the worksheet that corresponds to the instructor's worksheet. All questions are to be read aloud to the students. The illustrations visually identify the <u>subject</u> of the questions and serve as clues in remembering them, but they do not provide answers to the questions. Answering the questions requires logic, reasoning and adequate verbal skills. Students should take turns answering the questions. Answers will vary and are correct if they are logical.

Why?

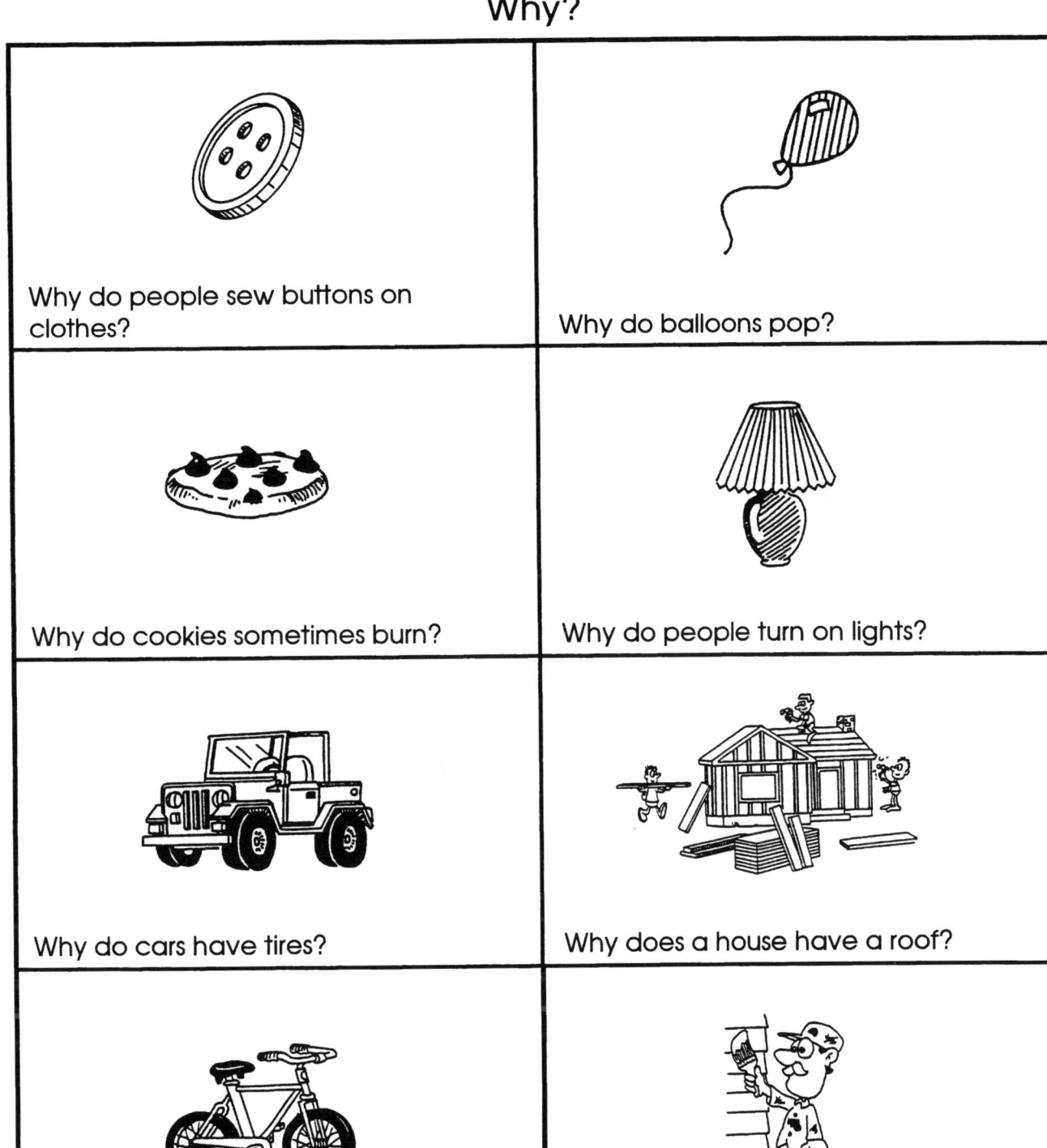

Why do people sew buttons on clothes?	Why do balloons pop?
Why do cookies sometimes burn?	Why do people turn on lights?
Why do cars have tires?	Why does a house have a roof?
Why are training wheels put on a bike?	Why don't you touch wet paint?

Great Ideas for Teaching, Inc.   <u>Verbal Reasoning Activities</u>

Name:_____

Why does this happen?

Great Ideas for Teaching, Inc. Page 21 Verbal Reasoning Activities

Instructor's Worksheet:

DIRECTIONS: Before beginning, each student should be given a copy of the worksheet that corresponds to the instructor's worksheet. All questions are to be read aloud to the students. The illustrations visually identify the <u>subject</u> of the questions and serve as clues in remembering them, but they do not provide answers to the questions. Answering the questions requires logic, reasoning and adequate verbal skills. Students should take turns answering the questions. Answers will vary and are correct if they are logical.

Why does this happen?

Why does a telephone ring?	Why does a saw need to be sharp?
Why does a jar have a lid?	Why do we need a ladder?
Why do we need rain?	Why do houses have doorbells?
Why does a school bus have so many seats?	Why does a teacher ask you to be quiet when she is talking?

Great Ideas for Teaching, Inc.   Verbal Reasoning Activities

Name: _____

Why does this happen?

Great Ideas for Teaching, Inc.   Verbal Reasoning Activities

Instructor's Worksheet:

DIRECTIONS: Before beginning, each student should be given a copy of the worksheet that corresponds to the instructor's worksheet. All questions are to be read aloud to the students. The illustrations visually identify the subject of the questions and serve as clues in remembering them, but they do not provide answers to the questions. Answering the questions requires logic, reasoning and adequate verbal skills. Students should take turns answering the questions. Answers will vary and are correct if they are logical.

Why does this happen?

Why do you eat soup?	Why do you keep milk cold?
Why do you store ice cream in a freezer?	Why do you dust your house?
Why do beds have pillows?	Why do people handle eggs very carefully?
Why do people watch TV?	Why do your parents work?

Great Ideas for Teaching, Inc.   Verbal Reasoning Activities

Name:_____

What would happen?

Instructor's Worksheet:

DIRECTIONS: Before beginning, each student should be given a copy of the worksheet that corresponds to the instructor's worksheet. All questions are to be read aloud to the students. The illustrations visually identify the <u>subject</u> of the questions and serve as clues in remembering them, but they do not provide answers to the questions. Answering the questions requires logic, reasoning and adequate verbal skills. Students should take turns answering the questions. Answers will vary and are correct if they are logical.

What would happen?

What would happen if you dropped a fish bowl?	What would happen if you dropped a ball?
What would happen if you left your socks out in the rain?	What would happen if you left a pail out in the rain?
What would happen if Mom forgot her house key?	What would happen if you made silly faces at a baby?
What would happen if a balloon hit something sharp?	What would happen if you picked some pretty flowers for your mother?

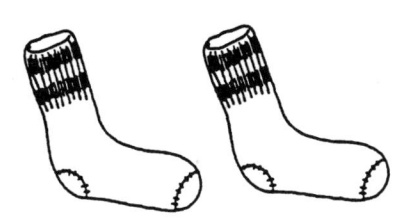

Great Ideas for Teaching, Inc.   Verbal Reasoning Activities

Name:_____

What would happen?

Great Ideas for Teaching, Inc.   Verbal Reasoning Activities

Instructor's Worksheet:

<u>DIRECTIONS:</u> Before beginning, each student should be given a copy of the worksheet that corresponds to the instructor's worksheet. All questions are to be read aloud to the students. The illustrations visually identify the <u>subject</u> of the questions and serve as clues in remembering them, but they do not provide answers to the questions. Answering the questions requires logic, reasoning and adequate verbal skills. Students should take turns answering the questions. Answers will vary and are correct if they are logical.

What would happen?

What would happen if you did not have any food?

What would happen if you did not have a car?

What would happen if you did not have a washing machine?

What would happen if you did not have a clothes dryer?

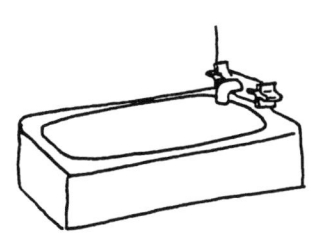

What would happen if you did not have a bathtub?

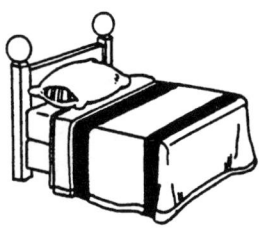

What would happen if you did not have a bed?

What would happen if you did not have a table?

What would happen if you did not have a chair?

Great Ideas for Teaching, Inc.   Page 28   <u>Verbal Reasoning Activities</u>

Name:_____

Why does this happen?

Great Ideas for Teaching, Inc.   Page 29   Verbal Reasoning Activities

Instructor's Worksheet:

DIRECTIONS: Before beginning, each student should be given a copy of the worksheet that corresponds to the instructor's worksheet. All questions are to be read aloud to the students. The illustrations visually identify the <u>subject</u> of the questions and serve as clues in remembering them, but they do not provide answers to the questions. Answering the questions requires logic, reasoning and adequate verbal skills. Students should take turns answering the questions. Answers will vary and are correct if they are logical.

Why does this happen?

Why is the girl turning the handle?

Why is the doctor taking an x-ray?

Why is the boy in a hospital?

Why is the girl holding a toothbrush and toothpaste?

Why does a wallpaper hanger use a long pole?

Why did the man yell "ouch?"

Great Ideas for Teaching, Inc. Verbal Reasoning Activities

Name:_____

Why does this happen?

Great Ideas for Teaching, Inc.   Verbal Reasoning Activities

Instructor's Worksheet:

DIRECTIONS: Before beginning, each student should be given a copy of the worksheet that corresponds to the instructor's worksheet. All questions are to be read aloud to the students. The illustrations visually identify the subject of the questions and serve as clues in remembering them, but they do not provide answers to the questions. Answering the questions requires logic, reasoning and adequate verbal skills. Students should take turns answering the questions. Answers will vary and are correct if they are logical.

Why does this happen?

Why is she pointing to the thermometer?	Why is the boy putting money in the slot?
Why do sailboats have sails?	Why do children wear helmets when they ride on skateboards?
Why are steps rolled up to an airplane?	Why does a train have an engine?

Great Ideas for Teaching, Inc.   Verbal Reasoning Activities

Name: _____

Why?

Instructor's Worksheet:

DIRECTIONS: Before beginning, each student should be given a copy of the worksheet that corresponds to the instructor's worksheet. All questions are to be read aloud to the students. The illustrations visually identify the subject of the questions and serve as clues in remembering them, but they do not provide answers to the questions. Answering the questions requires logic, reasoning and adequate verbal skills. Students should take turns answering the questions. Answers will vary and are correct if they are logical.

Why?

Why do people need tape when they wrap presents?

Why do people need napkins when they eat?

Why do chickens lay their eggs in a nest?

Why is this lady wet?

Why do you think this girl is writing a thank-you note?

Why does a referee need a whistle?

Great Ideas for Teaching, Inc.   Verbal Reasoning Activities

Name:_____

Why?

Great Ideas for Teaching, Inc.   Verbal Reasoning Activities

Instructor's Worksheet:

DIRECTIONS: Before beginning, each student should be given a copy of the worksheet that corresponds to the instructor's worksheet. All questions are to be read aloud to the students. The illustrations visually identify the <u>subject</u> of the questions and serve as clues in remembering them, but they do not provide answers to the questions. Answering the questions requires logic, reasoning and adequate verbal skills. Students should take turns answering the questions. Answers will vary and are correct if they are logical.

Why?

Why do the bakers need a hot oven?

Why does a barber need scissors?

Why does a painter need to wear a hat?

Why is this man digging a hole?

Why does the girl need to wear mittens?

Why do thumbtacks have sharp points?

Great Ideas for Teaching, Inc.   Verbal Reasoning Activities

Why?

Instructor's Worksheet:

DIRECTIONS: Before beginning, each student should be given a copy of the worksheet that corresponds to the instructor's worksheet. All questions are to be read aloud to the students. The illustrations visually identify the subject of the questions and serve as clues in remembering them, but they do not provide answers to the questions. Answering the questions requires logic, reasoning and adequate verbal skills. Students should take turns answering the questions. Answers will vary and are correct if they are logical.

Why?

Why is the mother upset?	Why does a fireman use a hose?
Why does the man have a net?	Why do people carry umbrellas?
Why did the children spread out a picnic cloth?	Why does a dog wear a leash?

Great Ideas for Teaching, Inc. — Verbal Reasoning Activities

Name:_____

Why?

Great Ideas for Teaching, Inc. Verbal Reasoning Activities

Instructor's Worksheet:

DIRECTIONS: Before beginning, each student should be given a copy of the worksheet that corresponds to the instructor's worksheet. All questions are to be read aloud to the students. The illustrations visually identify the <u>subject</u> of the questions and serve as clues in remembering them, but they do not provide answers to the questions. Answering the questions requires logic, reasoning and adequate verbal skills. Students should take turns answering the questions. Answers will vary and are correct if they are logical.

Why?

Why is the boy putting money in the toll booth basket?

Why is the girl squeezing oranges?

Why does the boy have on a bathing suit?

Why is the boy holding on to the steering bar?

Why does the boy have a basket?

Why does the girl have on her nightgown?

Great Ideas for Teaching, Inc.   Verbal Reasoning Activities

Name: _____

Why?

Great Ideas for Teaching, Inc.　　　Page 41　　　Verbal Reasoning Activities

Instructor's Worksheet:

DIRECTIONS: Before beginning, each student should be given a copy of the worksheet that corresponds to the instructor's worksheet. All questions are to be read aloud to the students. The illustrations visually identify the <u>subject</u> of the questions and serve as clues in remembering them, but they do not provide answers to the questions. Answering the questions requires logic, reasoning and adequate verbal skills. Students should take turns answering the questions. Answers will vary and are correct if they are logical.

Why?

Why is the boy sitting in the shade of the tree?	Why is the girl holding onto the ropes?
Why does the iron need to be hot?	Why must the ice be frozen very hard?
Why is the man hot and tired?	Why is the ice melting?

Great Ideas for Teaching, Inc.   Page 42   Verbal Reasoning Activities

Why does this happen?

Instructor's Worksheet:

DIRECTIONS: Before beginning, each student should be given a copy of the worksheet that corresponds to the instructor's worksheet. All questions are to be read aloud to the students. The illustrations visually identify the <u>subject</u> of the questions and serve as clues in remembering them, but they do not provide answers to the questions. Answering the questions requires logic, reasoning and adequate verbal skills. Students should take turns answering the questions. Answers will vary and are correct if they are logical.

Why does this happen?

Why do people put on jackets before they go outside in winter?

Why do people wash their windows?

Why is the boy sharpening his pencil?

Why does the diaper have a pin?

Why does a bulldozer have a blade?

Why does the farmer need a hoe?

Great Ideas for Teaching, Inc.   Verbal Reasoning Activities

Name:_____

Why does this happen?

Great Ideas for Teaching, Inc.   Verbal Reasoning Activities

Instructor's Worksheet:

DIRECTIONS: Before beginning, each student should be given a copy of the worksheet that corresponds to the instructor's worksheet. All questions are to be read aloud to the students. The illustrations visually identify the <u>subject</u> of the questions and serve as clues in remembering them, but they do not provide answers to the questions. Answering the questions requires logic, reasoning and adequate verbal skills. Students should take turns answering the questions. Answers will vary and are correct if they are logical.

Why does this happen?

Why does the man need a lawn mower?

Why does the girl need a hair brush?

Why does her car need gas?

Why does the boy need to wash his dog?

Why does the boy look sick?

Why did the ice cream fall?

Great Ideas for Teaching, Inc.   Page 46   <u>Verbal Reasoning Activities</u>

Name: _____

Why?

Instructor's Worksheet:

DIRECTIONS: Before beginning, each student should be given a copy of the worksheet that corresponds to the instructor's worksheet. All questions are to be read aloud to the students. The illustrations visually identify the <u>subject</u> of the questions and serve as clues in remembering them, but they do not provide answers to the questions. Answering the questions requires logic, reasoning and adequate verbal skills. Students should take turns answering the questions. Answers will vary and are correct if they are logical.

Why?

Why did the man pick up the meat with his fork?

Why is the girl turning on the lamp?

Why is the mother putting the baby in the carriage?

Why does the man need a knife?

Why did the man open the cash register?

Why is the bag around the bottom of the tree?

Great Ideas for Teaching, Inc.   Verbal Reasoning Activities

Name:_____

Why?

Instructor's Worksheet:

DIRECTIONS: Before beginning, each student should be given a copy of the worksheet that corresponds to the instructor's worksheet. All questions are to be read aloud to the students. The illustrations visually identify the <u>subject</u> of the questions and serve as clues in remembering them, but they do not provide answers to the questions. Answering the questions requires logic, reasoning and adequate verbal skills. Students should take turns answering the questions. Answers will vary and are correct if they are logical.

Why?

Why is the boy holding up one foot?	Why does the girl have crayons?
Why did the man buy ketchup?	Why is the girl looking out of the window?
Why is smoke coming out of the chimney?	Why should people not step on crabs?

Great Ideas for Teaching, Inc.   Page 50   <u>Verbal Reasoning Activities</u>

Name:_____

Why is this happening?

Great Ideas for Teaching, Inc.   Verbal Reasoning Activities

Instructor's Worksheet:

DIRECTIONS: Before beginning, each student should be given a copy of the worksheet that corresponds to the instructor's worksheet. All questions are to be read aloud to the students. The illustrations visually identify the subject of the questions and serve as clues in remembering them, but they do not provide answers to the questions. Answering the questions requires logic, reasoning and adequate verbal skills. Students should take turns answering the questions. Answers will vary and are correct if they are logical.

Why is this happening?

Why is the man putting on a costume?

Why is the man walking with crutches?

Why does the man have a brush?

Why is the man holding a fishing pole?

Why is the man signaling to the taxi driver?

Why is the man running?

Great Ideas for Teaching, Inc.   Verbal Reasoning Activities

Name:_____

Why?

Great Ideas for Teaching, Inc.   Verbal Reasoning Activities

Instructor's Worksheet:

DIRECTIONS: Before beginning, each student should be given a copy of the worksheet that corresponds to the instructor's worksheet. All questions are to be read aloud to the students. The illustrations visually identify the subject of the questions and serve as clues in remembering them, but they do not provide answers to the questions. Answering the questions requires logic, reasoning and adequate verbal skills. Students should take turns answering the questions. Answers will vary and are correct if they are logical.

Why?

Why does the pitcher have a ball?

Why is the farmer angry?

Why is the boy rolling the dice?

Why is the man pinning clothes on the line?

Why will this little boy's mother be upset when she sees him?

Why is the boy pushing the button?

Great Ideas for Teaching, Inc.   Verbal Reasoning Activities

Name:_____

Why?

Instructor's Worksheet:

DIRECTIONS: Before beginning, each student should be given a copy of the worksheet that corresponds to the instructor's worksheet. All questions are to be read aloud to the students. The illustrations visually identify the <u>subject</u> of the questions and serve as clues in remembering them, but they do not provide answers to the questions. Answering the questions requires logic, reasoning and adequate verbal skills. Students should take turns answering the questions. Answers will vary and are correct if they are logical.

Why?

Why is the girl washing dishes?	Why is the boy dropping glue on the paper?
Why does the man need a paddle?	Why do children put frosting on a cake?
Why is the man lighting a fire?	Why did the man put a fence around the garden?

Great Ideas for Teaching, Inc. — Verbal Reasoning Activities

Name:_____

Why do you think this is happening?

Great Ideas for Teaching, Inc.   Verbal Reasoning Activities

Instructor's Worksheet:

DIRECTIONS: Before beginning, each student should be given a copy of the worksheet that corresponds to the instructor's worksheet. All questions are to be read aloud to the students. The illustrations visually identify the <u>subject</u> of the questions and serve as clues in remembering them, but they do not provide answers to the questions. Answering the questions requires logic, reasoning and adequate verbal skills. Students should take turns answering the questions. Answers will vary and are correct if they are logical.

Why do you think this is happening?

Why do you think the boy is nudging his friend?

Why do you think the boy is filling the pitcher?

Why do you think the mother is telling her son not to eat the cupcake now?

Why do you think the girl needs the hammer?

Why do you think the man is waving?

Why do you think the boy is holding up his hand?

Great Ideas for Teaching, Inc.   Verbal Reasoning Activities

Why?

Instructor's Worksheet:

DIRECTIONS: Before beginning, each student should be given a copy of the worksheet that corresponds to the instructor's worksheet. All questions are to be read aloud to the students. The illustrations visually identify the subject of the questions and serve as clues in remembering them, but they do not provide answers to the questions. Answering the questions requires logic, reasoning and adequate verbal skills. Students should take turns answering the questions. Answers will vary and are correct if they are logical.

Why?

Why is the lady watering the plant?

Why is the baby crying?

Why is the lady using a hair dryer?

Why is the boy telling the dog to "Sh-h-h-h?"

Why is the man running?

Why do carpenters need lumber?

Great Ideas for Teaching, Inc.   Verbal Reasoning Activities

Name:_____

Why does this happen?

Great Ideas for Teaching, Inc.   Page 61   <u>Verbal Reasoning Activities</u>

Instructor's Worksheet:

DIRECTIONS: Before beginning, each student should be given a copy of the worksheet that corresponds to the instructor's worksheet. All questions are to be read aloud to the students. The illustrations visually identify the <u>subject</u> of the questions and serve as clues in remembering them, but they do not provide answers to the questions. Answering the questions requires logic, reasoning and adequate verbal skills. Students should take turns answering the questions. Answers will vary and are correct if they are logical.

Why does this happen?

Why does the man have a key?

Why does the boy need to go to bed early?

Why does the boy need a broom with a short handle?

Why does the man use an eraser?

Why do people put up mailboxes?

Why does the girl need a dish cloth?

Great Ideas for Teaching, Inc.   Verbal Reasoning Activities

Why does this happen?

Instructor's Worksheet:

DIRECTIONS: Before beginning, each student should be given a copy of the worksheet that corresponds to the instructor's worksheet. All questions are to be read aloud to the students. The illustrations visually identify the <u>subject</u> of the questions and serve as clues in remembering them, but they do not provide answers to the questions. Answering the questions requires logic, reasoning and adequate verbal skills. Students should take turns answering the questions. Answers will vary and are correct if they are logical.

Why does this happen?

Why do you think the boy is giving the girl a present?

Why do you think the boy's mother put extra covers on the bed?

Why do you think the girl is reaching for a pen?

Why do you think the girl is putting money in the savings bank?

Why does the man need to rake?

Why do you think the baker is baking cookies?

Great Ideas for Teaching, Inc.   Verbal Reasoning Activities